Re-Defining STRESS
to Prevent Disease

Re-Defining STRESS to Prevent Disease

CHANGING THOUGHTS, PERCEPTIONS AND
LEARNED EXPERIENCES FOR IMPROVED HEALTH

STEVEN JAFFE, MSNH

THE MIND DIET GROUP, INC.
Palm Desert, California

© 2006 Steven Jaffe

The Mind Diet Group, Inc
Phone: 760-613-1591
E-mail: Aminddiet@aol.com
Website: www.minddiet.com
www.aminddiet.com

All rights reserved. This book may not be reproduced in whole or in part, stored in a retrieval system, or transmitted in any form or by any means electronic, mechanical, or other without written permission from the publisher, except by a reviewer, who may quote brief passages in a review.

Mind Diet®, is a registered trademark of MDG, the Mind Diet Group, Inc. and should not be used or reproduced without written permission from the owner. When referred to in an article or review, the trademark symbol must appear.

Re-Defining Stress To Prevent Disease reflects the views, research, and personal experience of the author. This book is not intended as a guide to independent self-healing or diagnosis. No medical claim is made to the effect or outcome of the stress-reducing techniques described in this book.

Jaffe, Steven.

    Re-defining stress to prevent disease: changing thoughts, perceptions and learned experiences for improved health / Steven Jaffe. -- Palm Desert, Calif. : Mind Diet Group, 2006.

    p. ; cm.

    ISBN-13: 978-0-9720605-8-5
    ISBN-10: 0-9720605-8-8
    Includes bibliographical references and index.

    1. Stress management. 2. Medicine, Preventive. 3. Stress (Psychology)--Prevention. 4. Stress (Physiology)--Prevention. I. Title.

RA785 .J34 2006   2006926753
155.9/042--dc22   0607

Printed and bound in the United States of America
10 9 8 7 6 5 4 3 2 1

Cover and interior design by To The Point Solutions
www.tothepointsolutions.com

Contents

	Preface	7
	Acknowledgments	9
	Introduction	11
Chapter 1	How Stress Affects the Body	19
Chapter 2	The Symptoms of Stress	27
Chapter 3	Sources of Stress	31
Chapter 4	The Prevalence of Stress in Western Society	35
Chapter 5	Personality Characteristics, Stress and Disease	39
Chapter 6	Diseases Linked to Stress	43
Chapter 7	Stress-Coping Strategies	49
Chapter 8	Re-Defining Stress	55
Chapter 9	Dealing With Cognitive Stress Factors	59
Chapter 10	Solutions Available to Re-Define Stress	73
	Final Thoughts	81
	References	85
	Index	89
	About the Author	91

Preface

FOR THE LAST SEVEN YEARS I have been fascinated with stress and its affects on human health. Before I wrote this book, my focus for dealing with chronic stress was through a form of poetic therapy I named "self-talk" poetry. Subsequently, I wrote four poetic therapy books in my Mind Diet Series to treat the emotional effects of cancer, heart disease, relationships, and loss. My goal has always been to teach people how to cope and manage stress on a daily basis using writing as their vehicle to better emotional health.

Since my initial focus on writing and its effect on stress, I wanted to take my research to another level: to determine how using traditional stress reduction methods worked in combination with my poetry therapy technique. What I discovered was that the incorporation of at least one additional stress reduction technique with my program improved a person's capacity to be successful on the way to a specific goal.

We all need assistance in managing stress. It might be support for sticking to a plan to lose weight or dealing with an emotional condition during a life-threatening illness. It could be help improving romantic relationships or coping with one that is no longer in one's life.

Stress can be mitigated by adding meditation, yoga, or proper breathing techniques into a person's daily routine. The addition of "self-talk poetry" into that routine further enhances one's chance of reducing stress that can harm the body.

I have a strong conviction that a consistent form of "self-talk" writing, either in poetic form or simple prose, can be the catalyst for a long-lasting solution in preventing disease from entering a person's body. In fact, I believe that "self-talk" writing has the power of reversing the emotional complications stress has on an existing illness.

In this book, *Re-Defining Stress to Prevent Disease*, I have broadened my focus of reducing stress so as to examine how stress on the body, both emotional and physical, affects human health. The data will reflect how thoughts, perceptions, and learned experiences contribute to disease and illness. Numerous solutions to combat stress will be highlighted to reflect the many opportunities available to an individual to be able to live with joy and happiness, in a world filled with stress.

Re-Defining Stress to Prevent Disease looks at the methods available to reduce stress, and how by Re-Defining the way the brain interprets stress (cognitive stress), will allow the body to become balanced. This return to normal homeostasis can prevent disease. After reading *Re-Defining Stress to Prevent Disease*, the final decision on choosing the right course of action is solely up to the individual.

Acknowledgments

I AM SO GRATEFUL TO the many people who have been in my life to influence and guide me in the direction that led to me to finding poetry as my personal means for stress reduction.

I personally want to thank my wife, Nancy, for her support and encouragement during some of my most stressful times and showing me that through my written thoughts, everything in life can be attainable no matter how bleak things might seem at the time. Also, thank you for being the ear I needed and the red pen that helped me edit this book.

I want to thank Clayton College for helping me expand my horizons and discover a whole new world, which has shown me that the body can heal itself naturally and that quality of life is so much more fun than just living a long life.

Introduction

THIS BOOK WILL ANALYZE the causes of stress and how thoughts, perceptions and learned experiences contribute to disease and illness. Information discussed will explore how stress affects the human body and the methods that can be used to reduce stress by Re-Defining (re-framing) how the brain interprets stress, which will allow the body to become balanced and prevent disease.

Stress is everywhere. By definition it is the non-specific response of the body to any demand made upon it. All humans, both adults and children, experience stress. From dealing with a cranky boss, demanding parents, bullies at school, coping with the loss of a loved one or financial worries, stress is impossible to avoid. Stress can be acute, such as how the body reacts in the face of danger, or it can be chronic when a person is dealing with long-term stressful situations.

The body has a natural mechanism to cope with stress and when allowed to return to homeostasis, a person can function relatively disease free. However, stress is not easy to control. Usually the body's breakdown is the first signal that a person is suffering from severe stress. There are limited studies of the incidence of stress (as opposed to anxiety or depression), making it important for people to understand the effects of stress on the body.

The cognitive long-term results of stress have been linked to the development of many physical illnesses and diseases. Chronic stress can weaken the immune system and, conversely, the reduction of stress can help to strengthen the immune system. Stress can be conceptualized as a four stage cycle: thoughts, emotions, chemical reactions, and physical symptoms. It is not the pressures in one's life that cause stress. It is the way a person thinks about them. Epictetus, in 120 AD, believed that man is not disturbed by things, but by the views he takes of them. Thousands of years later, man has gotten worse in dealing with stress. Humans continue to remain caught up with unhealthy thoughts, perceptions and learned reasoning, which has led to an epidemic of stress in Western Society.

People have the ability to either create stress or reverse it. Like a professional athlete who can either psyche himself/ herself up for a win or a loss, it is this same process that a person can accomplish to control cognitive stress and keep the body in a state of homeostasis. The body's response to stress can produce the same arteriosclerosis risk that results from smoking or high cholesterol levels. This condition drastically increases the risk of heart disease and stroke.

Stress has also been linked to the development and progression of cancer, since it reduces the body's natural ability to seek out and destroy malignant cells. Mental

INTRODUCTION

stress also makes it more difficult to withstand the exhausting treatments often required to treat cancer, such as chemotherapy and radiation. Other diseases that are associated with stress include type II diabetes, ulcers, respiratory dysfunction, infections, and depression.

Stress is the body's natural mechanism to protect itself. With the enormous amount of pressures life has to offer, it has become a crutch that is driving millions of people unnecessarily to their doctors with stress-related illnesses. The brain is the origination point of stress and the main organ in the body that dictates whether a person will be healthy or ill.

When humans are experiencing a sense of "well-being" a "normal" amount of endorphins is present in the brain. However, when experiencing stress, the level of endorphins drops significantly. Some researchers estimate that the amount of stress in society doubles every ten years. The bottom line is that if stress levels do not seek their normal balance, the output of endorphins cannot return to equilibrium. Eventually, while under chronic stress, endorphin levels will keep lowering, creating poor health.

Releasing the sense of over-urgency in a person's life often becomes an ideal rather than a reality. People who create a more serene life and discover more enriching ways to live often have a better life (Carrington, 2001). Throughout history stress has been recognized as a force that seriously needs to be addressed. Unfortunately, teaching people to control stress can be unprofitable for doctors and pharmaceutical companies who make their living treating, instead of curing. It is the purpose of this paper to show people that there are remedies they can do on their own to improve their health.

However, the problem of stress is not that simple. Constant exposure to stressors in life has altered our brain, which in turn has altered the body's ability to maintain a homeostasis state. Human cells have a memory, and when chronic stress is not given the time to recede, the body will not return to equilibrium. The immune system reacts to any form of stress. Over time, unrelieved stress will seriously break down the immune system, eventually opening the body up to illness and disease.

Nowadays, people are bombarded with what might be called the belief system of stress, which suggests that psychological and physiological well-being is constantly threatened by degrees of stress unparalleled in history. However, nothing could be further from the truth. Life has always been historically stressful. What has changed is how humans cope with stress. Stress changes the way a person perceives the world: it affects one's senses, memory, judgment, and behavior (Martin 1997). It is important to understand the infectious nature of stress and how it seduces a person to crave it.

Managing stress can be complicated and confusing. There are different types of stress—acute, episodic, and chronic—each having its own characteristics, symptoms, duration, and treatment approaches. It is the myriad of stress that hinders a person's ability to get a handle on its management. It is hard to compare the stress humans faced thousands of years ago with today's situations. What can be analyzed today is the effects cognitive stress has on the body. The difference now is that humans have

INTRODUCTION

lost the ability to manage everyday pressures, which has elevated their perceptions to interpret that their hectic lifestyles are a signal for survival. Perceptions and learned experiences are totally out of skew and need to be brought back in line to allow the body to regain its ability to become balanced and healthy. I will attempt to show that once a person has an understanding of their unique stressors, how their individual perceptions and learned experiences control them, and the effects stress has on their body, they can direct the mind to re-define stress and bring the body back to an equilibrium state.

Re-Defining STRESS
to Prevent Disease

Chapter 1

How Stress Affects the Body

TO UNDERSTAND HOW STRESS affects the body, one has to be familiar with the three types of stress that bombard the mind and body: Acute, episodic, and chronic. Acute stress is the most common form of stress. It comes from demands and pressures that are connected to the past and a perceived future. Episodic stress is an elevated form of acute stress. People suffering this form of stress are in chaos and crisis a majority of their daily lives. Chronic stress usually originates from traumatic early childhood experiences that become painfully internalized and remain painful and with the person into adulthood (Miller & Smith, 1997).

Acute stress can be thrilling and exciting in small doses. This form of stress does not have enough time to do the extensive damage associated with long-term stress (Miller & Smith, 1997). Some symptoms are: anger, irritability, anxiety, depression, muscular problems, back pain, jaw pain, stomach and bowel problems, heartburn, acid stomach, flatulence, diarrhea, constipation, elevated blood pressure, rapid heart beat, heart palpitations, dizziness, migraine headaches, cold hands or feet, shortness of breath and chest pain (Miller & Smith, 1997).

Episodic acute stress is found in people who suffer acute stress frequently (Miller & Smith, 1997). They are people who are ceaseless worriers. The cardiac prone Type A personality fits into this category. Symptoms of episodic acute stress are: episodes of extended arousal, persistent tension head-aches, migraines, hypertension, chest pain and heart disease.

Chronic stress, unlike acute and episodic, is more serious and requires immediate intervention. This form of stress wears away at people day after day. Chronic stress is when a person never sees a way out of a desolate situation (Miller & Smith, 1997). This unrelenting demand on the body eventually puts a person in a situation that prevents them from seeing a light at the end of the tunnel. In most chronic stress situations all avenues of hope appear eliminated (Miller & Smith, 1997). The one distinguishing aspect of chronic stress is that people can get used to it. Chronic stress kills through suicide, violence, heart attack, stroke and perhaps even cancer (Miller & Smith, 1997).

The conscious mind can remain unaware of the different levels of stress that it is experiencing, triggering the body's defense mechanisms to silently fight off the effects of stress. Without awareness, a person cannot take the necessary measures to control stress. It is widely believed that the brain controls every organ in the body during a stressful event through the release of chemical hormones. Chemicals produced by the brain during an emotional crisis trigger the immune system to react, causing a spiraling effect that begins to break down the body's natural ability to seek homeostasis.

For example, cancer is the third most common cause of death in the Western world (Myss, 1997). Human beings produce cancer cells daily (Myss, 1997). The question is what triggers the cancer cells to become deadly (Myss, 1997). There are strong correlations with chemical toxins, genetics, excessive radiation, nutrition, viral infections and depression (Myss, 1997).

To most scientists and clinicians, the evidence points to depression and how it clobbers the immune system. It has been widely reported that cancer often is diagnosed one to two years following a devastating emotional crisis (Myss, 1993).

Stress has a powerful affect on the body. A person's full understanding of the consequences that stress offers is something people have to address, especially when fighting a life-threatening illness.

The two main biological systems involved in mediating the stress response are the sympathetic nervous system and the hypothalamus-pituitary-adrenal system. The normal role of the sympathetic nervous system is to mediate the unconscious regulation of basic bodily functions. In stressful situations it is also the chief mediator of the body's immediate alarm reaction—the so-called fight-or-flight response (Martin 1997). When the body maintains a constant state of stress, this condition will negatively impact the body's health. People need to learn how to take a time out, to retrain those memory cells by helping the brain reinterpret past stressful events.

Stress and tension are stored in the body, which results in tight shoulders, a stiff neck, backaches, headaches and more. If the physical tension is let go, a feeling of calm will help to handle the stress. Just telling the mind to let go is not enough. Reframing of cognitive stress has to take place in order to reverse or reduce stress. There are intimate links between our minds and the healing capabilities that we all inherit at birth (Miller, 1997). The exercise of journaling and addressing negative thoughts can help to reframe the brains thought process and in turn make significant positive changes in one's emotional health.

The relationship between thoughts, emotions, and the immune system can be explained in physiological terms. When one thinks a thought or feels a feeling, it communicates itself to every cell in the body by way of small protein molecule messengers called *neuropeptides*. In turn, the hormonal level of the body fluctuates according to one's emotional state.

Thoughts are toxic, and can kill or cure (Siegel, 1989). When humans experience mind-altering processes—for example, meditation, hypnosis, visualization, psychotherapy, love and peace of mind—humans become open to the possibility of change and healing (Siegel, 1989). How a person perceives stress has a dramatic effect on the production of immune molecules in the bloodstream, as well as certain immune cells via messages from the hypothalamus, the control center of the brain. It does not distinguish between positive stress and negative stress; thus the brain reacts by releasing a chemical response. If people are to heal themselves and others, it can be just as important to identify certain mental factors as it is to identify the physiological factors of illness (Miller, 1997). In some cases good stress can also be problematic. The body recognizes both eustress and distress as change, and it is change that causes the problem. The pace of change is so fast in today's society that few are untouched by it.

Some changes may appear beneficial on the surface, yet have negative aspects that become apparent later. A common example is the rapid increase in personal communication devices such as cell phones and pagers. At first glance they seem like marvelous devices that can enhance productivity by enabling more convenient communication with others. This may also work against a person's emotional health. As a society this modern convenience can become invasive. Employers may expect their workers to be "on call" constantly, and it becomes difficult to find quiet time to think, plan, or even to do the primary part of the job. Customers may not respect the difference between the workday and private time, and a person's family life feels the effect.

Stress can also come from physical and emotional sources. Physical causes can include—but are not limited to—overwork, over exercising, excessive partying, jet lag, toxins (such as air pollution and chemicals encountered at work or home), allergies, sleep deprivation, illness, injury and hormonal disruptions in the premenstrual, postpartum and menopausal phases of women's lives. When stress happens in a person's life, it is automatically assessed mentally. The body will not become imbalanced until the brain gives the orders to react. Thus, the brain first tries to determine if the event is threatening, the beginning stages of the stress response.

There are people who have good coping skills and will move through the stressful event easily. It is when a person believes that the immediate stressful event is beyond their coping skills that harmful chronic stress will take over. The key to controlling stress is to be able to see it clearly and understand the reactions the body is making during an emotionally disturbing event.

For the brain to cope with stress, a reappraisal of the problem needs to happen. For example, when a person feels a headache coming on they could take a moment to think about what is going on in their lives at that moment. They will more than likely see the stress that is affecting their body. By just recognizing it, giving it acknowledgment, they will begin the reversing process helping the headache to subside. This simple technique can be incorporated through the journaling process, meditation, deep breathing exercises, or slow relaxing walks.

Stressful situations can come from many everyday sources such as marital, family or peer relationship difficulties. Office politics, financial problems, moving or remodeling, juggling schedules of busy family members, taking care of aging parents or disabled children can also contribute to losing touch with the inner self, causing a host of other problems to ensue. Positive emotional events such as falling in love, getting married, having a baby, getting a raise or a new job, and graduating from school, all add to the difficulty of finding joy and happiness, which is a key ingredient toward reducing stress. All of these factors can contribute to long-term stress and cause or exacerbate many physical ailments.

There is a saying "if it is not broken, don't fix it." Unfortunately, humans live by that creed when it comes to taking care of their health. "What I don't know won't hurt me," has become a belief system for many hard-charging individuals. Unfortunately, when a person encounters stress, the body's own belief system automatically generates a biochemical reaction. Adrenaline or cortisol is then produced to enable the body to have the energy needed for the appropriate defensive action, which is selected from the well known Fight or Flight Response. (This is actually comprised of five choices: fighting, fleeing, and freezing, feeding or mating.) This is intended to be a temporary state of affairs.

The human body is designed to function best under conditions of predictability and consistency, known as homeo- stasis. The normal body rhythms and sleep cycles are part of this equilibrium state. Stress, with its accompanying hormonal changes, disrupts the natural balance, and the body then has to work overtime to return to a state of stability.

In times of continuing stress, the body has to work harder and longer in its attempt to seek balance, and it will soon manifest a number of symptoms. The first to appear is usually some sort of sleep disruption. Other symptoms include decreased energy, increased aches and pains, (especially in the head, neck, shoulders and back), increased sensitivity to pain, and a vague sense of feeling unwell. Humans may also experience gastrointestinal problems such as an upset or nervous stomach, diarrhea or constipation. Anxiety, agitation, and panic attacks are also relatively common.

In attempts to cope, a person often instinctively resorts to counterproductive strategies such as an increase intake of simple sugars, caffeine, alcohol or tobacco; compulsive work or exercise patterns may also be developed. All of these strategies actually tend to increase the stress instead.

Stress, like beauty, is in the eye of the beholder. What acts as a stressor for one person may simply be a motivator for another individual. Everyone has a unique tolerance level.

Some stress is good for everyone—though that amount will vary for each individual. With no stress or very low levels, people become lethargic and lackadaisical—often performing at very low levels. Too much stress, however, also results in poor performance as people concentrate more on the stress and often become overwhelmed. With moderate levels of stress, people are generally spurred on to higher performance and are more motivated to produce at higher levels. That "moderate level" is unique to each person.

Chapter 2

The Symptoms of Stress

THE BRAIN'S PRIMARY JOB is to prioritize information relevant to human survival. An event, either physical or emotional, that implies the possibility of danger or a threat, whether real or imagined, signals the brain to prioritize that event as the only important action that needs handling at the moment. This form of processing is the foundation of stress.

Symptoms of stress can be physical, emotional or mental. The problem for the brain is that it cannot distinguish which is real or imagined. The physical signs of stress can be the pounding of the heart, headaches, sweaty palms, indigestion, skin rashes, shortness of breath, cold hands, sleeplessness, fatigue, nausea, diarrhea, tight muscles, and pain. The emotional signs of stress can be irritability, moodiness, depression, anxiousness, hostility, and nervousness. The mental signs are forgetfulness, loss of concentration, poor judgment, disorganization, fuzzy perception, being confused, lack of interest, math errors, not thinking clearly, and negative self-talk.

People in the workplace are struggling with a relatively new phenomenon of modern lifestyles: work-related stress. It has been reported that up to 90 percent of the doctor's visits are said to be stress-related. Nearly 50 percent of Western workers experience stress, and stress is expensive (Stagey, 2002). It cost businesses more than $300 billion in lost productivity last year (Stagey, 2002). For most people, work is a significant and meaningful feature of life, contributing around 25% toward a person's life. Work should provide structure, purpose, satisfaction, self-esteem and spending power. However, due to downsizing and economic uncertainty, the workplace has become a setting of stress and worry.

Some of the more common symptoms of stress include headaches, high blood pressure, and chronic tiredness or fatigue. In addition, indigestion, stomach upset and ulcers are frequent signs of job-related stress. Personality changes, mental disorders and depression can signal a problem with managing stress. Failure to deal with stress at an early stage can often lead to heart disease. In addition, pent up stress may manifest itself in anger and abuse (both physical and mental).

Stress may cause violence and vice versa. The rise in the number of incidents of work place aggression has been tied to the rise in stress. An important step toward Re-Defining stress is for a person to first recognize how they react to stress. Identifying the external and internal factors that create distress can include being aware of people, places, time of the year, month or day that is causing stress. Recognizing feelings of tiredness, hunger, boredom or simply loss of energy is a form of self-evaluation and an important step toward bringing the body back to its natural equilibrium.

Chapter 3

Sources of Stress

THERE ARE VARIOUS SOURCES of stress. They include: survival stress, internally generated stress, anxiety, stress due to change, family, relationships, environmental stressors, chemical and nutritional stressors, hormonal factors and work-related stress. The problem people face today is not only the stress that constantly surrounds them, but also the never-ending assault the above sources of stress have on their lives. When perception of the environment is greater than the perception of the ability to cope, a person is said to be under chronic stress.

Hundreds of years ago humans were basically concerned with survival stress, utilizing the body's natural response when threatened physically or emotionally. That is not the case in modern life. More people are now worrying about events beyond their control, causing unnecessary worry, anxiety, and depression. With more and more illnesses being linked to stress, it is obvious that the sources of stress are too overwhelming.

In today's world of downsizing and mergers, a fear of job loss is one of the biggest sources of stress for many employees. Larger numbers of people are experiencing stress from not having the appropriate knowledge, skills or abilities to perform their jobs. The seriousness of these stressors carries over into the family and other relationships.

A feeling of powerlessness causes stress for workers today. Giving employees responsibility without the accompanying authority creates an environment for stress. Some feel stressed when they remain in a job that does not fit them. Even the physical surroundings on the job may create stress. Less than ideal working conditions can be hazardous. Poor heating/cooling, poor lighting and too much noise all can be a breeding ground for stress.

Change itself and increasing global competition sets the stage for fear and uncertainty leading eventually to stress. A diverse workforce has led to differences and conflicts, which in turn leads to stress. It becomes extremely difficult to leave stressful work problems at the office, creating a spiraling effect that transfers into the home.

The increase in dual-career families has resulted in more work/home conflicts. Elder care and child care issues are adding to the home stressors as well. People are finding themselves responsible not only for the care of aging parents, but also the upbringing of children, while at the same time trying to fulfill the obligations of a full-time job.

Keeping lines of communication open can often help minimize job-related stress. The inability to verbalize anxiety, fears, and worries keeps stress locked inside the workers mind. An important step toward reducing work-related stress is to talk with peers, loved ones or to get professional help.

Chapter 4

The Prevalence of Stress in Western Society

PEOPLE IN WESTERN SOCIETY live hectic lives. It seems to prime them for creating stress in their lives. Americans especially, are competitive, which in itself creates more stress. In this competitive culture, people tend to go without spirituality, allowing stress to penetrate into the everyday workings that Westerners call living. As heart disease and cancer continue to be on the rise in Western society, one of the links being stress, adjustment to everyday habits that are creating stress should be addressed.

A preponderance toward being stressed has become commonplace. It has become a billion-dollar industry that promises relief for something that is self imposed. Evidence is beginning to indicate that women may be more psychologically predisposed to the stressful effects of life events than men (Donoghue, 1999). One of the factors associated with these conclusions includes the multiple roles that women generally face that can lead to a variety of daily stressors contributing to depression (Donoghue, 1999).

In addition, women's social roles have been found to be associated with more ongoing stress than those of men (Golding, Potts & Aneshensel, 1991). For example, among married people, women do more household work than men. Housework is strongly associated with household strain among women, especially when it is combined with full-time work or the role of raising children. These multiple roles also appear to expose women to vicarious experiences of stress. For example, Mendes de Leon and Markides (2000) found that women experienced more negative life events than men. However, these differences did not result solely from the number of events directly occurring to the respondents themselves. Rather, women were exposed to a greater number of events that occurred to others, particularly their spouses. Golding et al.'s (1991) findings with a Western sample also revealed that people experience strain when life events involving job loss and subsequent economic strain happen not only to that person, but also to someone important to them (for example, spouse and family dependents). Unacknowledged stressful events can factor in accounting for psychological distress among women.

Women may be affected more adversely by marital stress and lack of marital social support, because they not only experience their own stressors, but also have disproportionate exposure to stressors of their spouse or partner and children. For Western females, although they may experience vivid sources of stress inside—and outside—

the home, they may tend to report these stressors as relating to the family and marital-relationship, that is, the home domain. On the basis of a strong adherence to familism, Latina females are expected to perform multiple tasks that are reinforced by strict sex-role expectations such as "keeping the peace" within the family, organizing family members' tasks, providing care giving for youths and infirm family members, maintaining religious and cultural rituals, providing health care activities, and so forth (Meadows, 1999).

Chapter 5

Personality Characteristics, Stress and Disease

ONE'S PERSONALITY CHARACTERISTICS are believed to be linked to many diseases, especially heart disease. Traits like hostility, ambitiousness, and impatience are at the core of heart disease. Like a set of fingerprints, a stress response by one individual will be uniquely different from another individual.

What causes one person to stress out can be a relaxation aid for another. Research has found a link between personality types and their reactions to stress. There are basically two types of personality traits: Type A and Type B.

What is a Type A or Type B personality? Unfortunately, there is not a broad stroke definition that fits everyone. In generalities, Type A personalities are highly competitive, very time oriented, in a continuous state of turmoil, have a tendency to watch the clock, have a desire to strongly hold to their opinions and fight change. By contrast, Type B personalities show a tendency toward being less competitive, taking more time to do things, and are more flexible.

Personality types do not indicate who will be more or less stressed. It depends on how the stressor is perceived. For example, if a Type A person creates competitiveness and then thrives off of it, enjoying the "rush" and "drive" that come along with it—they are experiencing eustress (good stress) and using it to their advantage. By contrast, if a Type B person tries to reduce competitiveness and cannot—they can stress out and fail utterly. How these personality traits affect the health of the individual has mixed opinions. Being aware of how one is reacting to a problem will bring to the surface any stress they are experiencing so they can make the necessary changes to keep their bodies in balance.

Research in the field of stress-illness relationships has invariably indicated that stressful life events do not have an invariant or universal impact on the health status of individuals (Rabkin & Streuning, 2002), and that the causal link between one's exposure to stress and subsequent likelihood of illness is typically weak (Rabkin & Streuning, 2002). Of particular interest are lines of research that focus on individuals who do not become physically or emotionally impaired in the face of major stressful events. These stress-resistant individuals are said to have resistance resources, such as social support, personality traits, and coping styles, which mediate or moderate the stress-illness relationships (Kobasa, 2000).

In a seminal study, Kobasa (2000) proposed the personality construct of hardiness based on the findings that not all business executives, as highly stressed men, fell sick under stress. Hardiness represents a general orientation toward self and world expressive of commitment, control, and challenge. Specifically, hardy men are committed to what they are doing in various areas of their lives; they believe in having some measures of control over the causes and solutions of problems; and they view changes in life and demands for adjustment as challenges and opportunities. Kobasa argued that such an orientation of hardy men would serve through positive appraisals and successful coping to mitigate the potential unhealthy effects of stress and prevent the organismic strain that often resulted in illness.

The concept of hardy men falls short of proving that stress does not affect men who appear strong and in control. Heart disease is the number one killer of men in the United States. This disease does not play favorites with men in middle management roles verses men that are in upper management. Stress knows no boundaries and affects the human body eventually. Most successful businessmen fall into the Type A personality trait standard and Friedman and Rosenman's (1974) research showed direct links between heart disease and the Type A personality. They formed a hypothesis that 28 percent of Type A men had clinical signs of heart disease compared with only 4 percent of the non-type A men (Friedman & Rosenman, 1974).

Depending on a person's personality trait there remains a need to be aware of how the body is dealing with stressors. Perceptions and personality go hand-in-hand and even though a person is a hardy personality type does not mean chronic stress will not affect his/her immune system. Personality trait can be hard to change. Understanding one's personality shortcomings and modifying how they perceive a situation is a positive approach to remaining successful without suffering the ill effects of stress.

Just as there are different personality traits, there are different ways to cope with stress. A constant dose of negative stress can affect the mind and body. The important thing is that one re-awakens the strength and joy inside (Roxanne, 1999). Exercise, proper nutrition, and spiritual reflection are good combatants for negative stress.

Chapter 6

Diseases Linked to Stress

STRESS IS AN UNCHECKED part of human life. It comes from mental or emotional activity, as well as physical activity. The counter productivity of emotional stress can cause physical illness, such as high blood pressure, ulcers, or even a heart attack. Physical stress from work or exercise is not likely to cause such ailments. It is a person's thought process, perceptions and past learned experiences that affect one's health. Every organ in the body can be activated by chemical hormones produced by stress. It is these hormones that create physical symptoms within the body.

Humans are equipped with their own unique stress response quotient (extent of coping ability), and when it is coupled with physiological and emotional responses, a spiraling chain of events can bring about disease and illnesses. What compounds this problem is when emotional stress (cognitive stress) becomes chronic or particularly frustrating, not allowing the body to ease up and return to homeostasis.

Recognizing the early signs of distress, and creating a plan to modify the way the brain interprets a particular stressor, can influence a person's survival. Stress has been linked to the number one killer of Americans each year, heart disease. The September 27, 2004 issue of *Newsweek* cited a September 2004 study in the *Lancet*. Researchers surveyed more than 11,000 heart-attack sufferers from 52 countries and found that in the year before their heart attacks, the patients had been under significantly more stress than some 13,000 healthy control subjects.

"Severe stress didn't pose as great a risk as smoking," admits Dr. Salim Yusuf of McMaster University, senior investigator on the study. "But it was comparable to risk factors like hypertension and abdominal obesity. That's much greater than thought before" (Underwood, 2004, p.54).

At every stage of heart disease, state of mind appears to play a role (Underwood, 2004). It is important to note that to explain the various effects the mind plays in all of this can be linked to stress. Humans still utilize the fight-or-flight response to stressful situations, except it is not used for life or death situations. The brain has been conditioned to interpret personal conflicts, pressures at work, relationship problems, and rush hour traffic as a serious danger. This thought process awakens the Hypothalamus, Pituitary and Adrenal glands sending them into battle looking for a foreign enemy that is attacking the body. Over time, health problems will materialize.

DISEASES LINKED TO STRESS

Experts define stress as an individual's response to a strong stimulus. But while most people view stress as being detrimental to a sense of well-being, it need not be. In fact, stress sometimes produces beneficial effects. For example, a writer facing a looming deadline might harness the associated stress to become more productive or creative. On the other hand, stress often takes a heavy toll on people's lives. Here are some other facts associated with stress:

- Stress generally follows a cycle referred to as the General Adaptation Syndrome, which is characterized by stages of alarm, resistance and exhaustion. The term "burnout" describes the feeling of exhaustion that may develop when someone experiences too much stress for an extended period of time.

- If the source of the stress cannot be eliminated, stress can be managed through exercise, relaxation, time management and support groups. Organizations can help employees cope with stress through wellness programs, stress-management programs, health-promotion programs and fitness programs.

- Work-related stressors fall into one of four categories—task, physical, role and interpersonal demands. Task demands are associated with the task itself (for example, an air traffic controller). Physical demands are stressors associated with the job setting. Role demands are stressors associated with job duties. Interpersonal demands are stressors associated with relationships that confront people in organizations.

Researchers are beginning to find insights into the mind's ability to heal the body. The problem is that people have become so sensitized to any stressful situation that the brain cannot relax long enough to return the body back to a balanced state. The use of placebos in medicine has been around for years. The tricking of the brain (placebo effect) has been, in some cases, shown to improve a person's health. In fact, it can be a soothing emotional experience, or be a distraction that can alter, in the positive, one's health.

At Duke University, researchers found that religious observance is associated with lower rates of illness and hospitalization (Underwood, 2004). In studies of HIV-positive men, researchers at UCLA have found that optimism is associated with stronger immune-cell function (Underwood, 2004). Also, research at Harvard suggests that the "relaxation response", a deep sense of calm experienced through yoga, prayer, or deep breathing exercises, can help counter the effects of chronic stress (Underwood, 2004). When the body is deeply relaxed it produces more nitric oxide and this can be an antidote to cortisol and other potentially toxic stress hormones.

For most people, stressful life circumstances are unavoidable. Why people find it easier to remain in a chronic stressed state has no clear answers. Stress is a condition that can become a habit. Even when the evidence points to the to stressful life circumstances such as poverty and discrimination, these circumstances can after years of suffering seem normal. Not everyone in poverty, or exposed to discrimination, experiences chronic stress. It becomes a matter of understanding life's unpleasant circumstances and seeing them for what they truly are: misguided perceptions. Once a clear picture of the stressor is acknowledged, change can begin to happen.

Other causes of stress are illnesses that often elude conventional medicine. The medical community attempts to fix the symptoms, not the cause of what a person is experiencing. This lack of understanding can lead to negative escalating consequences of stress include withdrawal behaviors (absenteeism, tardiness, less focus on work, poor concentration), as well the costs related to stress diseases, which may be behavioral, psychological or medical. Behaviorally, stress may lead to detrimental or harmful actions, such as smoking, alcoholism, overeating, drug abuse, accident proneness and violence. Psychological consequences of stress include sleep disturbances, depression, family problems and sexual dysfunction. Medical consequences of stress include heart disease, stroke, headaches, backaches, ulcers, skin conditions, diabetes, and migraine headaches (Miller, 1999).

Mind-body approaches to healing offers a more reasonable place to start in treating stress-related illnesses. The ultimate negative consequence of chronic stress is, of course, death. In the high-pressure world of Japanese business, for example, death from overwork, a syndrome called *karoshi*, claims 30,000 victims a year. The truth is that all people will experience stressful periods in their lives. How each stressor is handled can mean the difference between having good health or poor health. While conventional medicine can alleviate the symptoms of stress-based illnesses, these prescription drugs and medical treatments may have dangerous side affects. More importantly these treatments do not get at the cause of the stress. A mind-body approach for a stress remedy on the other hand has the advantage of doing no harm.

Chapter 7

Stress-Coping Strategies

THE ABILITY TO RE-DEFINE STRESS requires a deliberate effort to change one's perception of a situation. This is where the problem for most people begins and ends. A person's internal monologue is continual, automatic, and occurs partially outside of awareness (Jacobs, 2004). This monologue usually consists of negative distorted thoughts called Negative Automatic Thoughts-NATs (Jacobs, 2004). NATs are unconscious reactions to stress. A solution to changing the emotional responses to stress is through the practice of Cognitive Restructuring. Simply put, CR helps a person minimize the tunnel vision and false alarms the brain sets off in the stress response process. CR helps a person become more aware of their reactions to stress by being turned into their own negative internal monologue.

How can one make changes to their thinking, perceptions and learned experiences that will be ever-lasting ensuring a minimum of harmful stress in life? To understand that stress is a matter of perception is a first step. Writing about a stressful event helps a person to recognize the reality of the stress they are experiencing. A person's writing can include such questions as: is the thought really true? What is the worst thing that could happen? Is there another way to look at this situation? If I had one month to live, how important would this be? Am I using words like "never", "always", "worst", "terrible", or "horrible", to describe the situation (Jacobs, 2004). The simple act of journaling brings the unconscious cognitive stress to the surface, giving the brain an opportunity to read and interpret the reality of the stress being experienced.

Some people rarely feel stress, while others are crippled by it. Some stress is to be expected. It is a signal alerting a person to a situation that is of some concern. Stress can be a positive force in a person's life. Many roads to success are laden with difficulties. Everyone experiences stress. Those who say they are never stressed are probably not recognizing the symptoms. Avoiding stress is not the answer. The key is finding a solution.

Time management often heads the list of coping strategies for most people. Yet time management can be considered a misnomer because it really entails self-management. No one can create more time. One can just get better at managing the same allotted twenty-four hours a day.

How many times a day does someone utter that worn out phrase, "If only I had more time...?" Yet in most cases, it is not that they needed more time, they simply misused the time they had. Time itself is the troublemaker if not used properly. The inappropriate use of time often creates new stressors.

Some of the easier stress reducers include getting a sufficient amount of sleep and exercising. Simple exercising reduces pressure. It doesn't necessarily have to be a regimented exercise program—it can be as easy as walking. A balanced diet is important in reducing stress, as is limiting the amount of alcohol and caffeine in the diet.

Planning also helps in reducing stress. Realistic, reasonable goals are critical in stress management; the very act of setting unrealistic goals sets people up for stress and failure. Alternatives also have to be planned. People should have a Plan B ready or a back door in the event the original plan does not work out.

Learning to say no has been successful for many people. There is an inordinate amount of stress that comes with saying yes and then being sorry. Saying yes can often be the easy way out initially, but then stress results as the realization that agreeing to something unpleasant sets in, can make what was an attempt to be cooperative, a burden.

Letting go of aggravations is a coping strategy everyone can use. That is, when a stressful event has occurred or an unpleasant situation has arisen, people must deal with it and move on. To constantly relive the event and rehash the details prolongs the stress. Prioritizing is important in managing stress. Each person must recognize what is controllable and what is not. Those events not within the individual's control must be let go. That frees up time and energy to deal with those events that are within their control. The act of making a list of things on a person's mind is an easy-to-accomplish stress reducer. Having a list of stress items removes them from the thought process, providing needed relief to an already overworked brain.

Sometimes stress can build to unmanageable levels as a result of the cumulative nature of stress. To combat this, it often works to simply take a break from the stressful situation itself. One medically proven method is to journal about the stressful event. Somehow, when the individual returns to the situation, they are refreshed and the situation does not seem quite as bad as before. In addition, realizing that most stressful decisions do not need to be dealt with immediately, is a powerful intervention. Allowing a day or two to mull over a stressful decision can allow a negative perception to become a positive one.

Finding out what causes the way a person reacts to a stressful event can be enlightening. Journaling has been medically proven to help show a person the way, and is often a primary prescription to relieving the onset of acute stress. Journaling does not take a lot of thought or time-consuming effort. This process will help eliminate the words "stressed out" and make them disappear from the vocabulary.

While there are numerous strategies for turning stress into success, here are seven that can be helpful:

1. Make a conscious decision to manage stress. Be willing to change and to be open to new habits.

2. When facing a stressful event or issue, understand that suffering can result in wisdom. Let the stress become a motivation to expand mentally, emotionally and physically.

3. Move from thinking to doing. When feeling stressed out, analyze why this has happened. Take inventory by asking questions, such as: What is happening to me? What conflicts am I experiencing? What pressures, frustrations, and changes need acknowledging? What is it that makes me feel afraid, tense, depressed, alarmed? Then take that data and move from worry to action, from thinking to doing. Journaling is a powerful tool that can help discover important answers to negative problems. Writing provides a sense of control and allows the brain to become actively involved in solving problems rather than creating them.

4. Turn threats into challenges. When facing a crisis step outside of it for a moment and see the big picture first. Look for the opportunities, not the dangers.

5. Verbalize and ventilate. Find people to confide in. Telling and retelling one's story is an effective way to reduce stress and release negatively charged feelings.

6. Eat something nutritious. Low blood sugar, or not having enough fuel, can hinder the body's ability to cope with stress.

7. Make a list of the top five stressors going on at the moment. Attempt to write about them in the first person. This is a good way for self-talk, which is a key ingredient in seeing what is truly happening at the moment.

Chapter 8

Re-Defining Stress

RE-DEFINING STRESS CAN be a powerful tool for understanding why a person experiences various moods. By Re-Defining stress it helps challenge and rewrites the thinking that lies behind the stress in a person's life. Stress cannot be controlled until a person learns how to approach a negative situation in a positive frame of mind.

Productive Re-Defining stress strategies include identifying various sources of stress in one's life, and then removing those which are within one's control. The first step may be to see a family physician to rule out hidden illness that may be masquerading as stress. This can include diabetes, anemia, and thyroid, liver or kidney problems. The process of re-framing one's thoughts and perceptions is a rational and reliable method to discover if one's interpretations of a situation are correct and appropriate.

In addition to what the brain contributes to the stress process, there are other outside factors that need to be addressed. It becomes important to learn to say "no" to excessive work or social demands. One can set boundaries to protect personal time by postponing or canceling optional activities. Managing allergies and decreasing exposure to toxins will work in reducing stress on the body's organs. Eating well to control fluctuations in blood sugar, and reducing the pace of change will also control stress.

The next important step in Re-Defining stress is to find constructive ways of dealing with the stressors that cannot easily be removed. Changing the way a person thinks about a situation, and attempting to change one's mood when a stressful event is happening, can be accomplished through the journaling process. In order to re-define one's stress a creative process, such as writing about a stressful situation, allows a person to read one's thoughts and have the ability to go back and measure one's progress. This process allows for positive change and this type of change is one of the key ingredients in Re-Defining stress. In situations that cannot be resolved by writing, counseling or psychotherapy can help identify buried or denied emotional needs that aren't being met. It can also facilitate the development of successful coping strategies and different ways of perceiving each stressful situation.

Relaxation training, yoga, music therapy, and meditation can also be helpful, as are some of the holistic healing arts such as aromatherapy, reflexology, reiki, and massage therapy, energy balancing and emotional acupressure. No single approach will meet everyone's needs for every situation. They are all part of a healing prescription to bring the body back into balance. The objective is to learn how to nurture the mind and to re-type the way each stressor is perceived. It is important to note that these approaches will only temporarily reduce negative stress, rather than eliminate the unhealthy effects that stress is causing.

A more permanent way to reduce stress is to modify a person's thinking, perceptions, and past learned experiences. This approach can train the brain to better deal with recurring stressful events in one's life. When stress crops up again, as it is bound to happen, modifying one's thought process will allow the body to remain in a more balanced state. The act of writing uses the left brain-right brain approach to understanding the stressors in one's life. This course of action engages the left-brain and right-brain simultaneously keeping one in an analytical state, while at the same time opening the right-brain to the creative answers that will become enlightening (Hogan, 2003). Written communication to one's self offers the mind an opportunity for self-observation, gaining awareness, letting go, getting centered and taking action from the heart. Without a balanced mind, the body cannot remain healthy (Hogan, 2003). Even though writing is a powerful tool to reduce and re-type stress, a person should incorporate exercise, good nutrition, and meditation to help the body return to a healthy homeostasis state.

The process of Re-Defining stress is a useful tool for understanding one's moods and actions during stressful situations. Without a clear understanding of what lies behind a person's stress, performance on the job will be hindered, relationships will become strained and overall self-worth will be diminished. Learning to slow down and step back during a stressful situation will give the brain enough time to interpret if the event warrants immediate action.

Chapter 9

Dealing With Cognitive Stress Factors

CHRONIC STRESS ORIGINATES INSIDE a person's thinking, perceptions and learned experiences. How one handled stress in the past does not mean it has to be handled that way in the future. Stress coping skills are learned, and can be relearned changing how a person deals with stress.

The vast majority of modern day illnesses and diseases are a result of actions and behaviors (Miller, 1997). More physicians today accept the theory that the mind and emotions can have a negative affect on human health (Miller, 1997). An important question one should ask is: Can we teach people mental skills that stimulate the immune system to fight infection or cancer? Evidence from both laboratory studies and clinical practice indicates that in most cases the answer is yes (Miller, 1997). If a person's thoughts and perceptions are powerful enough to create illness and disease, then it should be possible to change those thoughts and perceptions to prevent disease and in some cases put a life-threatening illness in remission. Unfortunately, controlling stress has no easy solution and not everyone can, or is willing to, look deep into their emotions to bring their bodies back into a homeostasis state.

For those who find it hard to talk about stressful events, the simple act of writing out those thoughts can make a big difference. Writing about emotional experiences can release tension and improve physical and mental health (Ittayem & Cooley, 2005). Nida M. Ittayem and Eileen L. Cooley (2005), in a study at Agnes Scott College, compared narrative writing and drawing with a control writing condition for stress reduction. Thirty-four undergraduate women were randomly assigned to narrative writing, drawing, or control writing groups. Pre-and post-anxiety and stress levels were measured with the State-Trait Anxiety Inventory (STAI) (Spielberger, Lushene, Vagg & Jacobs, 1983); and the Subjective Units of Disturbance Scale (SUDS) (Wolpe & Lazarus, 1966).

A significant decrease in SUDS stress rating appeared in both narrative writing and drawing groups compared to an overall increase in the control group. No significant differences in pre-post STAI scores were found. Drawing and narrative writing may be equally effective in reducing stress (Ittayem & Cooley, 2005).

The *Journal of the American Medical Association* revealed that writing about stressful experiences can help reduce the symptoms of common diseases, such as asthma and rheumatoid arthritis. In the study entitled "Effects of Writing About Stressful Experiences on

Symptom Reduction in Patients With Asthma or Rheumatoid Arthritis," one group of patients was asked to write about their most stressful life experience for 20 minutes a day over three consecutive days. Another group was asked to spend an equal amount of time writing about their plans for the day. The results:

- Forty-seven percent of patients who wrote about their stressful experiences showed what physicians determined to be "clinically relevant improvement" in their conditions four months later.

- Only 24 percent of the second group showed a similar improvement.

This growing research has revealed that writing about one's thoughts and feelings can lead to:

- Improvements in immune functioning
- Fewer visits to the doctor
- An increased sense of well-being.

Commenting on the value of writing about stressful experiences as a stress-reduction technique, David Spiegel, M.D., in the Department of Psychiatry and Behavioral Sciences at Stanford University, wrote, "Ventilation of negative emotions, even just to an unknown reader, seems to have helped these patients acknowledge, bear, and put into perspective their distress."

In other words, "it is not simply mind over matter, but it is clear that mind matters." (National Alliance to Nurture the Aged and the Youth, 2002). The most common experiences written about by subjects of this study were the death of a loved one, relationship difficulties, a serious problem affecting someone close to them, and involvement in or witness to a car wreck or other disasters (National Alliance to Nurture the Aged and the Youth, 2002).

Other than writing about stressful events it is important to pay attention to diet. When stressed out, some people tend to overeat while others starve themselves. Both patterns sabotage stamina. Experts advise careful monitoring of eating habits during times of stress, making sure to consume a balanced diet from the four basic food groups: dairy, grains, meat, fruit and vegetables. Some recommend a vitamin supplement during periods of peak stress. Authorities caution against using fluids which contain caffeine.

The most critical element of stress management is to know how certain situations cause specific reactions. A person's thoughts can generate a negative stress cycle that can give the brain two commands. For example, a headache can affect moods and then in turn influence thoughts. Recognizing this pattern can teach the brain to learn to examine the stressful event and modify or change the automatic thoughts that accompany stressful events.

Dealing with cognitive stress can be overwhelming. The key issue about Re-Defining stress is to find a technique that allows feelings to be expressed. It is also important to discover the stress that triggers the brain, which in turn sends out chemical hormones that impair the immune system. Anxiety, feelings, frustrations, and negative thoughts should find a place outside of the mind. Writing about negative thoughts is a safe and proven method for accomplishing that task.

DEALING WITH COGNITIVE STRESS FACTORS

Stress has become so common that it is carried like a trophy. Stress reduction is big business. There are workshops, relaxation tapes, light and sound headsets, and hundreds of experts all dedicated to making a living helping people reduce stress. Stress has become the intimacy of the 21st Century. Caroline Myss, Ph.D., in her book, *Why People Don't Heal and How They Can*, uses a term, "Woundology," to explain the seductive powers of stress. People are not meant to stay wounded (stressed). They are supposed to move through tragedies and challenges and to help each other move through the many episodes of their lives. By remaining stuck in the power of one's wounds (stress), the ability for transformation is blocked (Myss, 1997).

People may respond to stress as a warm fuzzy friend, allowing the mind to become seduced by its familiarity. Breaking that cycle is the key component in Re-Defining stress. One can become sensitized, or acutely sensitive, to stress. Once that happens, even the slightest intimation of stress can trigger a cascade of chemical reactions in the brain and body that assault the body from within. A person can develop an emotional allergy to stress. While it is psychological, it is the equivalent of having a hay fever attack. When the brain becomes sensitized to stress, it only takes a small amount of stress to trigger a headache, stiff neck, asthma attack or fit of anger. Not all people have allergic reactions; but with the constant unrelenting demands from life, a majority of people are prone to chronic stress.

Stress habituation can be a callous friend. When the brain is sensitized to stress it allows the body to be hammered by stress chemical hormones, while at the same time keeping the person's perception about stress the same. It is as if the brain sees a pot of water and jerks the hand away believing it is boiling.

Because some stress is absolutely necessary in living creatures, everyone has a built-in gauge that controls reactions to it. It's a kind of biological thermostat that keeps the body from launching an all-out response literally over spilled milk. Being overly sensitive to any stressful situation creates an imbalance in the body, and as a result, the response typically reserved for life-threatening events is turned on by life's mundane aggravations. This situation may produce too many excitatory chemicals or too few calming ones; either of the responses are inappropriate. The revelation that stress itself alters our ability to cope opens the door to retraining the brain to react differently. The human quest to seek a balanced relaxed life is a goal of most people. What one wishes for and what one receives can be two different things. There are many outer and inner factors that prevent the body from warding off unhealthy stressors.

Pre-conditioning to stress may occur before one is old enough to prevent it themselves. A traumatic event experienced by a baby could condition the adult to react negatively to certain stressful situations. It is like having one's buttons pushed. With the understanding of how people respond to stress may also explain why people have different tolerances for stress. In the past, stress tolerance may have been chalked up to mental fortitude: "He's a rock," or "She's really bearing up under pressure," Now it's clear that a person's ability to withstand stress has less to do with whether they are strong-willed, than with how much and what kind of stress they encountered in the past.

In modern society, stress does not always let up. People constantly exhibit anxiety and worries about daily events and relationships. Stress hormones continue to flow through the system in high levels, permanently absorbed in the blood and tissues. The stress response that once gave ancient people the speed and endurance to escape life-threatening dangers runs constantly inside people today and never shuts down.

Whether a person is a stressed-out executive or a laid-back skier, humans all start out with the same biological machinery for responding to stress. Stress activates primitive regions of the brain, the same areas that control eating, aggression, and immune response. It switches on nerve circuits that ignite the body's fight-or-flight response as if there were a life-threatening danger.

The stress response (fight-or-flight response) is "wired" into the brain and has been part of the human anatomy since the cave-dwellers. What was once needed to deal with life-threatening situations is now being used to handle the normal pressures of life (non-life-threatening). The same fight-or-flight circuits are all working overtime in response to such varied stressors as extreme exercise, the death of a loved one, an approaching deadline, or a long line at the check-out stand.

The human body is slowly killing itself by responding to the stress of everyday life as if it was a major threat. The onslaught of chemical stress hormones wears away at the immune system, opening the way to cancer, infection, and disease. Hormones, unleashed by stress, eat at the digestive tract and lungs, promoting ulcers and asthma. They may weaken the heart, leading to strokes and heart disease.

Cognitive stress at all levels, acute, episodic acute stress and chronic, trigger the chemical stress hormones in the body. The process starts out in the hypothalamus, an area of the brain located near where the spine runs into the skull. The hypothalamus is closely connected with the nearby pituitary gland and the distant adrenal glands, perched atop the kidneys. The so-called hypothalamic pituitary axis (HPA) has virtually total control of basic body functions. It regulates blood pressure, heart rate, body temperature, sleep patterns, hunger and thirst, and reproductive functions, among many other activities.

The pituitary gland hangs off the hypothalamus waiting to receive instructions on which of its many hormones to release and in what quantity. The pituitary releases substances that regulate growth, sex, skin color, bone length, and muscle strength. It also releases adrenocorticotropin, a hormone that activates the third part of the body's stress system, the adrenal glands.

Stress triggers the communication between the hypothalamus and the pituitary ending at the adrenal glands. The HPA axis release the stress hormones—dopamine, epinephrine (also known as adrenaline), norepinephrine (noradrenaline), and especially cortisol. Reactive to the adrenal hormones are basic body functions like blood flow and breathing that even minute changes in levels of these substances can significantly affect health.

Further complications from stress can be exhibited in the slight overproduction of dopamine which can constrict blood vessels and raise blood pressure. In addition, a shift in epinephrine could precipitate diabetes, or asthma, by constricting tiny airways in the lungs. If the adrenal gland reduces cortisol production, the result may be obesity, heart disease, or osteoporosis; too much of the hormone can cause women to take on masculine traits like hair growth and muscle development and lead to one of the greatest fears of all for aging men—baldness. High levels of cortisol may kill off brain cells crucial for memory.

The adrenal gland is also home of all stress reactions, the fight-or-flight response. Sensing impending danger the hypothalamus presses out cortisol-releasing factor, a hormone that prompts the pituitary gland to release adrenocorticotropin (ACTH). Carried in the bloodstream to the adrenal glands, ACTH triggers production of cortisol and epinephrine. The end result of this hormonal relay is a sudden surge in blood sugar, heart rate, and blood pressure—everything the body needs to flee or confront the imminent danger.

While this response is necessary to protect the body, it should not be utilized as a normal response to everyday stressors. Over time the unnecessary release of these hormones will begin to harm the organs it was designed to protect, opening the body up to illness and disease.

The stress system is responsible for coordinating much more than just a response to stress. For example, cortisol directly impacts storage of short-term memory in the hippocampus. The stress hormones dopamine and epinephrine are also neurotransmitters widely active in enabling communication among brain cells.

Directly and indirectly, they act on numerous neural networks in the brain and throw off levels of other neurotransmitters.

Stress, it's now known, alters serotonin pathways. And

through effects on serotonin, stress is now linked with depression on one hand, aggression on the other.

Many new studies catalogue how even a little stress can have wide-ranging effects on the body. For example:

- Epinephrine, released by the adrenal glands in response to stress, instigates potentially damaging changes in blood cells.

- Other substances released in the stress response impair the body's ability to fight infections. An immune system thus suppressed can raise susceptibility to colds—or raise the risk of cancer.

- Cortisol activation can similarly damage the immune system. This breakdown is a direct link to why people get colds.

- Stress hormones are also implicated in rheumatoid arthritis. The hormone prolactin, released by the pituitary gland in response to stress, triggers cells that cause swelling in joints.

- After being released by the pituitary gland, the stress hormone ACTH can impede production of the body's natural pain relievers, endorphins, leading to a general feeling of discomfort and heightened pain after injury. High levels of ACTH also trigger excess serotonin, now linked to bursts of violent behavior.

What can now be measured is how stress affects all the organs of the body. This observation of biochemicals is exposing the exact lines of communication between mind and body. The dividing line between what is biological and what is psychological is being erased. Once people learn how to recognize the stress in their lives and how to positively interpret it will allow the human body to regain its natural ability to heal itself and stay healthy.

The challenge with dealing with stress is that stress does not work on a pre-defined schedule. Not everyone shows some immediate physical reaction to stress. Certainly, not all people suffer a heart attack or asthma attack when they get upset. Some seem able to take stress in their stride, while others routinely are overwhelmed. However, once a person feels the effect of chronic stress it is too late to prevent an illness or disease from entering the body. Looking at stress as a chemical reaction and realizing that this reaction can change how people react in the future can add enlightenment to many things witnessed regarding stress.

Stress begins inside the brain and in turn the brain triggers chemicals that affect the immune system. It seems logical that by altering one's perceptions of stressful events, one can alter the chemical reactions produced by the brain. One study that warrants further research is re-programming a person's stress response. If the brain can be taught to react differently to programmed thoughts, perceptions, and learned experiences, it follows that the elevation levels of hormonal chemicals released by the brain will be reduced, improving a person's overall health and prevent disease.

Stress requires the melding of disciplines ranging from genetics to psychology to medicine, and demands a new theory of mind/body interactions. Entirely new strategies to combat stress need to be considered to re-type stress.

Cognitive stress affects every aspect of human life, from the challenges of marriage, raising children in an environment of unparalleled peer pressure and drug abuse, to financial and work demand pressures. When left to spiral inside the brain, it increases anxiety levels, exacerbates anger and illness, and disrupts sleep patterns. Activity effectiveness is reduced and performance deteriorates rapidly, leading to mental and physical ill health and, in very extreme cases, to death.

From a business perspective, cognitive stress has profound negative impacts such as illness, absenteeism and, less visible, but equally damaging, bad decision-making, negative internal politics and communication and apathy. Absenteeism or negative activity generated by chronic stress can become one of the most rapid and damaging forces within an organization. Seemingly minor incidents can escalate causing a domino effect. The work performance of other employees collapses as each individual struggles to deal with overload caused by having to deal with their own workload and that of absentee colleagues.

The British Heart Foundation estimates that 21 percent of all sickness absence in the UK is due to stress-related heart disease, which apparently costs the average UK company with 10,000 employees, 73,000 working days lost, the death of 42 of its employees (between 35 and 65 years of age) and $7.5 million in lost production annually (Ganey, 2004).

Cognitive stress is a reaction to fear, and fear stops

people from taking action. Employees and managers who cannot take positive action when doing their jobs will cost corporations billions of dollars annually. A solution for managers and employees would be to focus on the emotions associated with each stressful reaction through writing, counseling, or communication with another person, which can bring the stressor to the surface and help retrain the brain.

The difficulty dealing with cognitive stress is that the human stress response is not so adaptive in today's hectic world. What is happening is that prolonged stress (chronic stress) stimulates the adrenal glands pumping out glucocorticoid hormones, which have the effect of suppressing the immune system opening the body up to disease (Martin, 1997). The immune system is a defensive system designed to keep the body healthy. Unfortunately, as the brain battles with cognitive stress, the immune system is trying to respond correctly to what the brain is telling it. It is a delicate balancing act that it does not get right during chronic stressful periods. The problem the body has is that as the brain provides the wrong signal, so does the immune system opening the body up to the harmful affects from bacteria, viruses or cancer cells. A person suffering from prolonged stress has a greater chance of getting a fatal disease compared to a person who has learned to deal with the stress in their lives.

An important step when dealing with stress is to recognize that any degree will be intertwined with a person's mental and physical health, especially in the chronic stress stage. A person needs to have a workable plan to modify their perceptions with the goal of changing their thinking and learned experiences, which will prevent the brain from overreacting to the stress response. It becomes important to reduce and eliminate the brain's reaction to stress and minimize the releasing of harmful toxic chemical hormones throughout the body, which can result in an unconscious form of suicide.

Chapter 10

Solutions Available to Re-Define Stress

UNDERSTANDING THAT OUR MINDS can damage our health, researchers, as well as medical professionals, continue to search for ways of improving a person's emotional and physical health. The pendulum is swinging back toward holistic approaches for mental healing. The curative powers of hypnosis, relaxation therapy, physical exercise and behavioral therapies are being prescribed as a primary step in reducing the harmful affects of stress. All types of stress are treatable. Here's a look at what helps:

PSYCHOTHERAPY: Cognitive behavior therapy (CBT) exposes one to anxiety-provoking situations in a controlled fashion, using relaxation techniques such as deep breathing, progressive muscle relaxation, or meditation. A recent study found that CBT worked just as well as antidepressant drugs for treating panic disorders.

EXPOSURE THERAPY: A form of desensitization therapy called exposure therapy is used to treat phobias and PTSD by bringing a person progressively closer to what she's afraid of, so she can learn to conquer her fear. A new virtual-reality version of the technique simulates the experience using a sensory headset.

NUTRITION: People with anxiety disorders are sensitive to body-chemistry changes that can result from food or drink intake. If a person gets hyped up or jittery after consuming caffeine, sugar, or alcohol, these should be avoided. Also to be avoided is long stretches of time without eating; doing so causes a drop in the blood-sugar level, which can bring on anxiety. Exercise Studies have shown that exercise (light or high-intensity) can reduce anxiety levels. (Miller, 1999)

YOGA: Is an ancient science of self-awareness. The practice of YOGA provides an experience of Oneness, empowers the practitioner with an inner strength, while fostering harmonious relationships with others. It creates a foundation of relaxation and peace mentally, physically, and emotionally. Numerous studies have demonstrated the powerful effect of exercise on the physical, mental, and emotional development of young people. YOGA exercises and postures are particularly useful as they work directly to reduce stress, strengthen the nervous system, and stabilize ones emotional foundation.

POETRY THERAPY: Poetry is a natural medicine (Fox, 1997). Poetry therapy provides guidance, revealing what one did not know before the poem was written. "This moment of surprising yourself with your own words of wisdom or of being surprised by the poems of others is at the heart of poetry therapy." (Fox, 1997). Poetry triggers the left-brain into action (the analytical part), allowing the right-brain (the creative part) to see the truth behind the stressful situation. Poetry therapy is the intentional use of the written and spoken word for healing and personal growth. The Website www.poetrytherapy.org provides links to poetry sites and training and education information. A Mentor list posted on their web site under Training and Education can be used to locate a poetry therapy practitioner in various geographical locations in the U.S. (Reich, 1999). The benefit of poetry is that it is a companion through dark times. The poem is a voice that makes it clear one is not alone. Whether reading or writing poetry, applying the lines of a poem to one's life experience helps uncover the meaning within questions, problems and cries (Fox, 1997).

JOURNALING: Scientific evidence supports that journaling provides other unexpected benefits. Writing about anger, sadness and other painful emotions helps to release the intensity of these feelings. The act of writing accesses the self-talk aspect of one's life, allowing the stressful negative thoughts to go from the brain to paper.

MEDITATION: This process significantly controls high blood pressure at levels comparable to widely used prescription drugs, and without the side effects of drugs. Hypertension decreases oxygen consumption, heart rate, respiratory rate, and blood pressure, and increases the intensity of alpha, theta, and delta brain waves, the opposite of the physiological changes that occur during the stress response.

MEDICATIONS: (This therapy method should be considered when all other therapies are not helping). Antidepressants and anti-anxiety medications, such as Buspar, have shown success with anxiety disorders. But in many cases, a combination of psychotherapy and medication is considered to be the best course of action to help a patient mentally defuse the situations that set off anxiety bombs.

Re-Defining stress is a process, not a one-step solution. Depending on the severity of one's stress, writing or using poetry to deal with difficult emotions should be utilized after some of the other stress reducing therapies have been practiced. Poetry and writing therapies work best when the mind is relaxed and opened to seeking out change. A person should evaluate their personal situation and determine the severity of their stress levels. It is important during the beginning stages of Re-Defining stress to find someone (a close friend or therapist) to discuss what is needed to reduce stress levels.

Stress is physical, especially cognitive stress, and it leaves signs throughout the body. When a person begins to experience physical reactions listed below, it is a signal that chronic stress is beginning to attack the body. Many physical ailments linked to stress can interfere with a person's desire for change, creating fatigue, exhaustion, and the desire to give up. The facts listed below are signals that stress is beginning to affect the body:

- Nine out of ten headaches are due to tension-caused muscle contractions in the neck and shoulders that radiate to the head.

SOLUTIONS FOR RE-DEFINING STRESS

- Stress creates forgetfulness, indecisiveness and poor concentration.

- Pupils dilate making vision slightly blurry but also expanding peripheral sight. Also, stress can cause spasmodic twitching of small muscles around the eye.

- Ears can start ringing or clicking, likely due to steady contraction in auditory muscles.

- Tension makes one unconsciously hunch their shoulders, causing muscle tightness and pain.

- Stress causes a person to take short, shallow breaths. When a person is anxious it deprives the lungs of oxygen. This causes the person to yawn—the body's way of forcing deeper breathing.

- Stress constricts blood vessels in the arms and legs while also increasing the heart rate. The combination results in a spike in blood pressure. Over time this will cause the arteries to become blocked, creating chest pains. If left unchecked this can led to a heart attack or stroke.

- Diarrhea, cramps, gas, and heartburn are all symptoms of irritable bowel syndrome, which may be brought on by anxiety.

- When stress levels climb, erections may fall, both because of the psychological effects of anxiety and because of the physical effects of constricting capillaries.

- Dandruff may proliferate in response to continued stress as a weakened immune system allows snow-making fungi to multiply.
- Chronic stress increases the chance for more colds and flus. Studies show that stress dampens immune response to viruses.
- Stress-induced surges of adrenaline can also make the nose red by dilating blood vessels.
- Saliva flows less freely, making the mouth and throat dry. Overtime, this can cut back on natural bacteria control and cause dental problems.
- Clenching the teeth can make muscles tight and provoke jaw pain.
- Stress causes a person to swallow more air, which leads to more belching.
- Stress produced adrenaline makes sweat glands pump out extra volumes of perspiration to cool the body.
- Stress hormones, called catecholamines, make blood thicker and more prone to clotting, increasing the risk of a heart attack.
- Stress hinders a person's natural ability to lose weight. The stress hormone cortisol encourages fat to dump into the midsection creating flab. A person suffering from chronic stress will

generally find that exercise and dieting are not producing the results they desire.

- Stress causes tight muscles in the lower back causing spasms, especially in backs strained from prolonged sitting.

- Stress increases bladder shyness, or difficulty relieving oneself in public restrooms when others are present.

- Extra sweating during stress robs the body of minerals that carry electrical signals to muscles, resulting in muscle cramps.

- Chemicals released by the nervous system can trigger reactions in skin cells, which in turn can provoke hives or psoriasis. Warts can also pop up under stressful conditions.

- Legs may start twitching, possibly due to stress-induced brain-chemical imbalances causing involuntary muscle contractions.

- Extra sweat and decreased blood volume to extremities make feet cold, wet and clammy.

Stress knows no boundaries and affects everyone. How people learn to deal with the stress in their lives will determine their overall health and performance, both in their career and relationships. A commitment toward change, a Re-Defining of how one perceives and reacts to stress, is a powerful solution to preventing disease.

People want life to be easy. By practicing some, or all, of the suggestions in this book will help toward a joyful and healthy life-style.

Final Thoughts

The relationship between the mind and health is juggled both by a person's thoughts and perceptions, as well as the biological connection between the brain and the immune system. This relationship is so delicate that the combination of daily stressors, along with the long-term conditioning of the brain contributes to poor emotional and physical health of people. The medical community can no longer think that the mind and body are not interlinked.

Dr. Hans Selye defined stress as essentially the rate of all wear and tear caused by life. Stress, then, is acting upon the individual by the external environment (Selye, 1950). Each person must take charge and be more proactive. A reactive stance to stress exacerbates the problem, often leaving one with a sense of helplessness (Selye, 1950).

Stress is good for everyone, although that amount will vary for each individual. With no stress, or very low levels, people become lethargic and lackadaisical, often performing at very low levels. Too much stress, however, also results in poor performance as people concentrate more on the stress and often become overwhelmed. With moderate levels of stress, people are generally spurred on to higher performance and are more motivated to produce at higher levels. That "moderate level" is unique to each person. Through the process of Re-Defining stress one can re-train the brain to find the right stress quotient that will work healthily for the individual. It is impossible to totally eliminate stress. One must learn how to better manage stress and the stressors that life presents. There are a number of coping strategies mentioned in this paper that can be used to help manage stress.

In the early part of the decade, the fastest growing category of workers' compensation claims was those for stress-related injuries. Employees are being bombarded with a variety of sources of stress—both in and outside the workplace. (Parachin, 2002). Now that companies have learned that it is critical to help their employees manage stress, the cost for claims is beginning to decrease.

Each person needs to take responsibility for their thinking, perceptions and learned experiences so they can become aware of the stress in their lives. Only then will they begin to re-type how they react to stressful situations. One must find the coping strategy or relaxation technique that works best for them. Some may find that a long walk relaxes and refreshes. Others may find tension is released if they write about the problem, read a good book, exercise, eat a balanced meal, or listen to music.

Sometimes the difference between managing stress successfully or unsuccessfully is just a matter of perspective. Those who are not handling stress well may need to change the way they view stress, and most importantly, change the way they react to the stress. Perhaps it is just a matter of not overreacting to stressful situations.

FINAL THOUGHTS

All stress is not created equal. There is both positive and negative stress. Positive stress spurs individuals on to higher performance and does not impact the individual's health as negatively. This is referred to as eustress. Negative stress is called distress. This is the more damaging stress that takes its toll on the individual. The damage to one's health is physical as well as psychological. This damage is not reversible. Once the body's system has responded to the negative stress—the damage is done. Over an extended period of time, this on and off again stress can be serious as the damage to one's health accumulates.

The key is for each person to recognize the signs of stress not only in themselves, but in those around them. Each individual needs to select coping strategies to help them better manage stress. This is an ongoing challenge. Stress is said to be the illness of this decade. No one can escape it. The best one can do is learn how to effectively manage stress. Re-Defining stress by using some or all of the methods mentioned in this book will help prevent disease or place a serious illness into remission.

References

Brown, R. (1999). How People under Pressure Cope with Stress. *Ebony.* Volume: 45. Issue: 9, 78.

Carrington, P. (2001) *The power of letting go.* London, England. Vega. introduction.

De Mello MF. Mirtazapine effectiveness in a patient with refractory psychotic depression. *Int J Psychiatry Clin Pract* 1999; 3(2):141-2

Dennis, B. (2004). Interrupt the stress cycle. *Natural Health*, Oct2004, Vol. 34 Issue 9, p70

Donoghue, C. (1999). *Positive Stress.* New Zealand Management, Jul2003, Vol. 50 Issue 6, p55

Fairbank J.A. (2002). Treatment of posttraumatic stress disorder: Evaluation of outcome with a behavioral code. Behavioral Modification, 7, 557-568.

Fox, J. (1997). Poetic Medicine, The Healing Art of Poem-Making. New York, NY. Penguin Putnam, Inc. p.3-5

Friedman M. & Rosenman R.H. (1974). *Type A Behavior and Your Heart.* New York, NY. Knopf.

Ganey, J. STRESS SOS. (2004). *Essence,* Vol. 35 Issue 3, p182.

Golding, J. M., Potts, M. K., & Aneshensel, C. S. (1991). Stress exposure among Mexican Americans and non-Hispanic whites. *Journal of Community Psychology,* 19, 37-58.

REFERENCES

Golino, S. (2004). Find Your Stress Spot. *Cosmopolitan*, Vol. 236 Issue 7, p178,

Hewitt P.L. (2003). The Multidimensional Perfectionism Scale: reliability, validity and psychometric properties in psychiatric samples. *Psychol Assess*; 3:464-8.

Hogan, E.E. (2003). *Way of the winding path*. San Francisco, CA. White Cloud Press. P.18

Ittayem, N.M. & Cooley, E.L. (2005). Self-Disclosure of Emotional Experiences: Narrative Writing and Drawing for Stress Reduction. *Psi Chi Journal*, Vol 9, issue 3. Agnes Scott College. Retrieved March 15, 2005 from http://psichi.org/pubs/articles/article 454.asp.

Jacobs, G. (2004). Using cognitive restructuring techniques to minimize the effects of stress on sleep. Retrieved December 7, 2004 from http://www.talkaboutsleep.com/sleepdisorders/insomnia_drjacobs_cognitiveRestructuringTechniques.html

Kobasa, S. C. (2000). Stressful life events, personality, and health: An inquiry into hardiness. *J. Pers. Soc. Psychol.* 37: 1-11.

Kobasa, S. C., & Maddi, S. R. (1977). *Existential personality theory*. In Corsini, R. J. (ed.), Current Personality Theories. F. E. Peacock, Itasca, IL.

Lauer, C.S. (2000). The three R's for stress. *Modern Healthcare*, 4/1/2002, Vol. 32 Issue 13, p27.

Martin, P. (1997). *The healing mind*. New York, NY. St Martins Press

Meadows EA. (1999). Psychosocial treatments for post-traumatic stress disorder: A critical review. In J. Spence, J.M. Darley, & D.J. Foss (Eds.), *Annual Review of Psychology*. Palo Alto, CA: Annual Reviews Inc., Vol. 48, pp. 449-480.

Mendes de Leon, C., & Markides, K. (2000). Depressive symptoms among Mexican Americans: A three generation study. *Journal of Epidemiology*, 127, 150-160.

REFERENCES

Miller, E. (1997). *Deep healing; the essence of mind body medicine.* San Rafael, CA. Hay House.

Miller, K.I. (1999). Communication and empathy as precursors to burnout among human service workers. *Commun Monogr;* 55:250-65.

Miller, L.H. & Smith, A.D. (1997) *The stress solution.* APA Help Center: Get the Facts: Psychology at Work: The Different Kinds of Stress. Retrieved June 27, 2004 from http://helping. apa.org/work/stress4.htm.

Mitchell, R. E., Cronkite, R. C., & Moos, R. H. (2003). Stress, coping, and depression among married couples. *Journal of Abnormal Psychology,* 92, 433-448.

Myss, C. (1997). *Why people don't heal and how they can.* New York, NY. Three Rivers Press.

National Alliance to Nurture the Aged and the Youth, (2002) *Stress Reduction Techniques.* Retrieved on March 15, 2005 at http://nanay.com/News%20Update/Nov%202001/Nov%202002/Stress.html

Parachin, V. M. (2002). Seven strategies for turning stress into success. *Supervision, Vol. 54 Issue 7, p6,*

Rabkin, J. G., & Streuning, E. L. (2002). Life events, stress and illness. *Science* 194: 1013-1020.

Ratcliffe, G. (2005). *Stress, a patient's guide.* Retrieved May 20, 2005 from http://www.medic8.com/healthguide/articles/stress.html

Reich, J. (1999). Comorbid anxiety and depression and personality disorder: a possible stress-induced personality disorder syndrome. *Psychiatr Ann;* 29(12):707 12

Selye, H. (1950). *The Physiology and Pathology of Exposure to Stress: A Treatise Based on the Concepts of the General Adaptation Syndrome and the Disease of Adaptation.* Medical Publishers, Montreal, Canada.

Siegel, B. (1989). *Peace, love, and healing.* New York, NY. Quill.

REFERENCES

Stagey, C. (2002). Is it more than just stress? *Marie Claire* (US), Vol. 9 Issue 12, p213.

Tyler, K. Cut the Stress. *HR Magazine,* May2003, Vol. 48 Issue 5, p101

Underwood, A. (2004). For a Happy Heart. *Newsweek,* September 27, 2004, p54

What to do about stress in your life. Tufts University Health & Nutrition Letter, Aug2000, Vol. 18 Issue 6, p5

Index

acid stomach 20
acupressure 56
acute stress 19, 52, 66
adrenal gland 44, 66-68, 71
adrenaline 25, 66, 78
adrenocorticotropin (ACTH) 67-68
aggression 65, 68
alcohol 51, 74
alcoholism 47
anger 19, 28, 63, 70, 75
anti-anxiety medications 76
antidepressants 76
anxiety 20, 26, 31, 33, 60, 62, 65, 70, 73-78
aromatherapy 56
asthma 60-61, 63, 65-66, 69

back pain 20, 22, 47, 79
balanced diet 51, 62
belching 78
blood pressure 20, 28, 43, 66, 75, 77
blood sugar 67
body rhythms 25
body's defense mechanisms 20

boredom 29
bowel irritation 20, 77
burnout 45

caffeine 51, 62, 74
cancer 21, 35, 59, 65, 68, 71
change 23, 32
chronic stress 12-14, 19-20, 24, 31, 41, 46-47, 59, 63, 69-71, 76-78
clenching teeth 78
cognitive behavior therapy 73
cognitive restructuring. 49
cognitive stress 22, 43, 50, 62, 66, 70-71, 76
cold hands 20, 27
colds 68
constipation 20, 26
coping skills 24, 59
cortisol 25, 46, 66, 67, 68, 78

dandruff 78
depression 20-21, 27-28, 31, 36, 47, 68
diarrhea 20, 25, 27, 77
distress 23, 28, 36, 44, 61, 83

INDEX

dizziness 20
dopamine 66-67
drug abuse 47, 70

elevated blood pressure 20
emotional crisis 21
endorphins 13, 68
epinephrine 66-68
episodic stress 19-20, 66
eustress 23, 40, 83
exercise 51, 73, 74
exposure therapy 74

fatigue 27-28, 76
fight or flight response 21, 25, 44, 65, 67
flatulence 20
forgetfulness 27, 77

gas 77
general adaptation syndrome 45
genetics 21, 69

happiness 24
headache 24, 27-28, 47, 62-63, 76
heart attacks 20, 43-44, 69, 77-78
heart disease 28, 35, 39, 41, 44, 47, 65, 67, 70
heart palpitations 20
heartburn 20, 77
hippocampus 67
hives 79
holistic approaches 73
homeostasis 11-12, 14, 21, 44, 57, 60

hormonal changes 25
hormonal chemicals 69
hypertension 20, 44, 75
hypnosis 22, 73
hypothalamic pituitary axis 66
hypothalamus 22, 44, 66-67
hypothalamus-pituitary-adrenal system 21

immune system 21-22, 59, 65, 68-69, 71, 78, 81, 93
indigestion 27-28
irritability 20, 27

jaw pain 20, 78
journal(ing) 24, 50, 52-53, 56, 75

karoshi 47

loss of concentration 27
low blood sugar 53
lower back pain 79

marital stress 36
massage therapy 56
medical consequence 47
meditation 22, 24, 56-57, 73, 75
migraine headaches 20, 47
mind-body approach 47-48
muscular problems 20
music therapy 56

nausea 27
Negative Automatic Thoughts-NATs 49

INDEX

neuropeptides 22
nutrition 21, 42, 57, 74

optimism 46
overeating 47, 62
overwork 23, 47

panic attacks 26
personality characteristics 39-40
phobias 74
physical illness 43
pituitary gland 44, 66-68
poetry therapy 74-76
prolactin 68
psoriasis 79
psychological consequences 47
psychotherapy 22, 56, 73, 76

reiki 56
relaxation therapy 73
religious observance 46

serotonin 67-68
shortness of breath 20, 27
short-term memory 67
skin rashes 27, 47
 hives or psoriasis 79
sleep cycles 25
sleeplessness 27
smoking 47
social demands 56
sources of stress 31
spirituality 35, 42
stomach irritation 20, 25, 28
stress, definition of 11
stress habituation 63

stress hormones 65-68, 78
stress-illness relationships 40
stress-related injuries 82
stress-related symptoms
 anger 19, 28, 63, 70, 75
 back pain 20, 22, 47, 79
 belching 78
 bowel irritation 20, 77
 clenching teeth 78
 cold hands 20, 27
 colds 68
 constipation 20, 26
 dandruff 78
 depression 20-21, 27-28, 31, 36, 47, 68
 diarrhea 20, 25, 27, 77
 dizziness 20
 fatigue 27-28, 76
 flatulence 20
 forgetfulness 27, 77
 gas 77
 headache 24, 27-28, 47, 62-63, 76
 heart palpitations 20
 heartburn 20, 77
 hives 79
 indigestion 27-28
 irritability 20, 27
 jaw pain 20, 78
 loss of concentration 27
 overeating 47, 62
 psoriasis 79
 skin rashes 27, 47
 sleeplessness 27
 stomach irritation 20, 25, 28
 sweating 79
 sweaty palms 27
 tight muscles 27, 79
 warts 79

stress-resistant individuals 40
stroke 12, 20, 47, 65, 77
sweating 79
sweaty palms 27
sympathetic nervous system 21
symptoms of stress 27, 28

teeth, clenching 78
tight muscles 27, 79
time management 50
toxic chemical hormones 72
toxins 23, 56
traumatic event 64
Type A personality 20, 39-41
Type B personality 39-40

violence 28, 47
visualization 22

warts 79
women (and stress) 35, 36, 60
work-related stress 28, 31, 33, 45
writing also see journaling 57, 60, 61, 62, 76

yoga 8, 46, 56, 74

About the Author

STEVE JAFFE, author, lecturer, and life-style coach, has a Master's degree in Natural Health and is presently completing his doctorate in the same field. A survivor of stress-related heart disease, he is living proof that stress can be re-defined and illness can be reversed.

Jaffe has been interviewed on over seventy-five radio and television stations around the United States and Canada and has published an article in Great Britain, "Poetry for Health and Healing."

His other Mind Diet® Series books include: *Count Your Life With Smiles, Not Tears*; *Healing From Within, Emotionally Surviving Cancer*; *A Recipe for Healing, Coming Together as a Team*; and *Beyond Valentine's Day, Making Love All Year Long* (which gained him the title from the Oakland Press as the "Most Romantic Man in the World").

Jaffe says, "Learning to understand stress and how conscious and unconscious stress affected my body was my first step in controlling my heart disease. Using my technique of "Self-Talk Poetry" has opened many positive new doors for me, which includes my passion of being a novelist. Once I learned to make stress my friend, I was able to pursue with enthusiasm and joy all the things that stress had once prevented me from accomplishing."

Since writing the first four books in his Mind Diet Series and two novels, Jaffe has discovered through his research that most people do not know how to live with stress. He believes this lack of understanding causes the immune system to attack the body's organs, which in turn creates disease and illness at staggering rates.

In this fifth book in The Mind Diet Series, *Re-Defining Stress to Prevent Disease*, Jaffe examines the causes of stress and how thoughts, perceptions, and learned experiences contribute to disease and illness.

The author lives with his wife, Nancy, in Palm Desert, California and can be reached at:

E-mail: Aminddiet@aol.com
Website: www.minddiet.com

Other Books in The Mind Diet® Series

Count Your Life With Smiles, Not Tears
Healing From Within, Emotionally Surviving Cancer
A Recipe for Healing, Coming Together as a Team
Beyond Valentine's Day, Making Love All Year Long

www.minddiet.com

www.ingramcontent.com/pod-product-compliance
Lightning Source LLC
Chambersburg PA
CBHW021020090426
42738CB00007B/845